About the Author

ALICE WALKER won the Pulitzer Prize and the American Book Award for her novel *The Color Purple.* Her other novels include *Now Is the Time to Open Your Heart, By the Light of My Father's Smile, Possessing the Secret of Joy,* and *In the Temple of My Familiar.* She is also the author of three collections of short stories, three collections of essays, six previous volumes of poetry, including *A Poem Traveled Down My Arm,* and several children's books. Born in Eatonton, Georgia, Walker now lives in northern California.

Also by Alice Walker

FICTION

Now Is the Time to Open Your Heart
The Way Forward Is with a Broken Heart
By the Light of My Father's Smile
Possessing the Secret of Joy
The Temple of My Familiar
The Color Purple
You Can't Keep a Good Woman Down
Meridian
In Love and Trouble: Stories of Black Women
The Third Life of Grange Copeland

NONFICTION

Sent By Earth: A Message from the Grandmother Spirit
Anything We Love Can Be Saved
The Same River Twice: Honoring the Difficult
Warrior Marks (with Pratibha Parmar)
Living by the Word
In Search of Our Mothers' Gardens

POEMS

A Poem Traveled Down My Arm
Her Blue Body Everything We Know
Horses Make a Landscape Look More Beautiful
Good Night, Willie Lee, I'll See You in the Morning
Revolutionary Petunias and Other Poems
Once

Absolute

Trust

in the

Goodness

of the

Earth

Random House Trade Paperbacks
New York

Absolute Trust in the Goodness of the Earth

New Poems

ALICE WALKER

2004 Random House Trade Paperback Edition

RANDOM HOUSE TRADE PAPERBACKS and colophon are
trademarks of Random House, Inc.

This work was originally published in hardcover by Random House,
an imprint of The Random House Publishing Group, a division of
Random House, Inc., in 2003.

Library of Congress Cataloging-in-Publication Data
Walker, Alice.
Absolute trust in the goodness of the earth: new poems /
Alice Walker.
p.   cm.
ISBN 0-8129-7105-1
I. Title.
PS3573.A425 A64 2003
811'.54—dc21   2002069990

The author is committed to preserving ancient forests and natural resources
and wishes to acknowledge Random House for printing this book on paper
that is 100 percent postconsumer recycled fibers and processed chlorine free.
For more information about Green Press Initiative and the use of recycled
paper in book publishing, visit www.greenpressinitiative.org.

Printed in the United States of America
Random House website address: www.atrandom.com

2   4   6   8   9   7   5   3   1

Book design by Mercedes Everett

Para "El Chinito" Guillermo,
and to the blessed Feminine
in us all

Let's admit it. We women are building a motherland; each with her own plot of soil eked from a night of dreams, a day of work. We are spreading this soil in larger and larger circles, slowly, slowly. One day it will be a continuous land, a resurrected land come back from the dead. *Mundo de la madre,* psychic motherworld, coexisting and coequal with all other worlds. This world is being made from our lives, our cries, our laughter, our bones. It is a world worth making, a world worth living in, a world in which there is a prevailing and decent wild sanity.

—*Clarissa Pinkola Estés, Ph.D.*

Preface

Most of these poems were written at Casa Madre, our ochre red house, my daughter's and mine, on the central coast in Mexico. I had moved out of the large white room with veranda looking toward the Pacific and into what is usually a guest bedroom. Smaller, darker, quieter; less yang, far, far more yin. It was shortly after the attacks on the World Trade Towers and the Pentagon; I was feeling a deep sadness about the events and an incredible weariness that once again whatever questions had been raised were to be answered by war. Each morning, after sitting for half an hour, I wrote several poems. This was something of a surprise, since I had spent the past couple of years telling my friends I would probably not be writing anything more. What will you do instead? one of them asked. I would like to become a wandering inspiration, I replied. I had an image of myself showing up wherever people gathered to express their determination to have a future or to celebrate the present, speaking, reading, playing one of my very simple musical instruments, and just being around. I did not think I needed to offer much more than this. I still don't. It is the best that I have and the easiest to give. Still, obviously, life had more writing for me in mind—if poems can actually be called writing. I have now written and published six volumes of poetry since my first collection, written while I was a student and published in 1968. From that first volume to this, what remains the same is the sense that, unlike "writing," poetry chooses when it will be expressed, how it will be expressed, and under what circumstances. Its requirements for existence remain mysterious. In its spontaneous, bare truthfulness, it bears a close relation to song and to prayer. I once told someone I could not have written my novel *The Temple of My Familiar* with straightened hair. I could not have written these poems in a bright sunny room where there were no shadows.

What many North Americans lost on September 11 is a self-centered innocence that had long grated on the nerves of the rest of the world. With time, more of this innocence will be shed, and this is not a bad thing. With compassion for our ignorance, we might still learn to feel our way among and through shockingly unfamiliar and unexpected shadows. To discover and endure a time of sorrow, yes, but also of determination to survive and thrive, of inspiration and of poems. The adventures one encounters will, of necessity, have a more risk-filled depth.

In my mid-fifties I devoted a year to the study of plant allies, seeking to understand their wisdom and to avail myself of the aid to insightful living that I believe the earth provides as surely as do meditation centers. I also wished to understand the ease with which so many in our Western culture become addicted: to drugs, to food, to sex, to thinness. What are we lacking that we so predictably can be sold all manner of harmful material in an effort to make up for it? I was particularly interested in discovering what our children are seeking when they turn to drugs and alcohol. Three times during the year I gathered in a circle with other women and a shaman and her assistant and drank *ayuascha,* a healing medicine used for thousands of years by the indigenous peoples of our hemisphere. *Ayuascha* is known as "the vine of the soul" and is considered holy.

With this assessment I completely agree; I remain awed by my experiences. Several times I gathered with both women and men for the eating of mushrooms, called by the people who use them for healing "flesh of the gods." For my final communication with the spirits of the plant world, at least in this form, I journeyed to the Amazon, home of "Grandmother" Ayuascha, where she herself instructed me I need look no further in her mirror; what she'd shown me already was enough.

As I see it, this is the work of the apprentice elder: to travel to those realms from which might come new (or ancient) visions of how humans might live peacefully and more lovingly upon the earth. I learned a lot, some of it fairly obvious. Our children take addictive drugs partly to allay their fears about what begins to look like a severely compromised future, one filled with hatred and with war. They take drugs to feel less lonely in a world that consistently chooses "profit" over community. But the most fundamental reason they take drugs, many of them, is the desire to have a religious or spiritual or ecstatic and transformative experience, a need hardwired into our being. Until relatively recently—the last five hundred years or so—most of our people had rituals during which they used all manner of inebriants to connect them with the divine. No one had invented a system to make money off of making others intoxicated. Nor were there laws forbidding the use of sacred plants used in healing and in ceremony—laws that, in the United States, have had a soul-killing effect on the native peoples whose connection to the infinite for thousands of years centered around the eating of mushrooms and particularly of peyote. I returned to my "ordinary" magical life much changed, and much the same, but deeply respectful of all our ancestors and their great inquisitiveness about, and belief in, the universe around them.

It was during these travels, internal ones and external ones, that I became aware of María Sabina, whose beloved face appears near the poem that invokes her name. Shaman, healer, priestess of the mushrooms, she was a legend in Mexico even while alive. Today she remains passionately revered, respected, loved, because she dedicated her life to the health and happiness of all humans. Whatever she is smoking will be used to cure whichever patient might be lying before her. She may receive a vision of what the illness is, or she may blow smoke over the sick person, purifying them and everything they touch. A poor Mazatec Indian from the mountains of Oaxaca, she has left a legacy of an amazing freedom, the foundation of which is absolute trust in the goodness of the earth; in its magic, in its love of us humans, in its ever present assistance the moment we give ourselves, unconditionally, into its wonder.

Woman who thunders am I, woman who sounds am I,
Spiderwoman am I, hummingbird woman am I,
Eagle woman am I,
Whirling woman of the whirlwind am I,
Woman of a sacred enchanted place am I,
Woman of the shooting stars am I.

—*María Sabina**

* From *Plants of the Gods: Their Sacred, Healing and Hallucinogenic Powers*, by Richard Evans Schultes, Albert Hofmann, and Christian Ratsch (Healing Arts Press).

Acknowledgments

I wish to thank Wendy Weil, Kate Medina, and
Jessica Kirshner for all their thoughtfulness
and help.

Contents

My Ancestors' Earnings

Not Children

The Award

The Backyard, Careyes

I Can Worship You

I Can Worship You

I can worship
You
But I cannot give
You everything.

If you cannot
Adore
This body.

If you cannot
Put your lips
To my
Clear water.

If you cannot
Rub bellies
With
My sun.

The Love of Bodies

Dearest One
Of flesh
& bone

There is in
My memory
Such a delight
In the recent feel of your warm body;
Your flesh, and remembrance of the miracle
Of bone,
The structure of
Your sturdy knee.

The softness of your belly
Curves
My hand;
Your back
Warms me.

Your tush, seen bottomless,
Is like a small,
Undefended
Country
In which is grown
Yellow
Melons.

It is such a blessing
To be born

Into these;
And what a use
To put
Them to.

To hold,
To cherish,
To delight.

The tree next door
Is losing
Its body
Today. They are cutting
It down, piece
By heavy piece
Returning,
With a thud,
To
The earth.

May she know peace
Eternal
Returning to
Her source
And
That her beauty
Lofty

Intimate
With air
& fog
Was seen
And bowed to

Until this
Transition.

I send love
And gratitude
That Life
Sent you
(And her)
To spend
This time
With me.

After the bombing of 9/11, September 25, 2001

All the Toys

You have all
The toys
& you keep them
To yourself.
Every once
In a while
Each hundred
Years
Or so
A few of us
Get a toy or two
& go skimming about the earth
Just like
You do.

But we feel
Foolish
Out there
In the blue sea
The crisp
White boat
Listing, lost
For all the world
To see.

We drift
Aimless
Just
Like you

Wondering
If toys is all
There is
To this game
Still wondering
As you seem
To
With all your
Toys
When will our ship
Come in.

Poem for Aneta Chapman
on Her 33rd Birthday

It's you
Who taught her
To read
She says
With soft eyes
Telling me
One
Of the many reasons
She cherishes
You.

Following her gaze
Into the past
I see two
Small
Sweet
Dark hands
Clasped
Two hooded
Tiny heads
Four
Ashy little
Legs
Bravely crossing
The wintry
Streets
Of Cleveland, Ohio

Destination:
Library.

You pause
At every corner
The littler hand
Secure
In your scarcely
Larger one.

Be careful
You say
With gentle
Emphasis.
We must wait
For the green light.

Aries
Holding on
To Cancer:
The one who
Leaps upon the world
Held safe
By
The one
Who
Stays home
To mind
The hearth.

Today
It is

Still
Your warm
Sure hand
She trusts
Your shy smile
That makes
Her happy
Your face
In the largest
Room
That
Makes her
Feel safe
&
Not alone.

You are the sister
The big
Sister
As hero.

The one who sees
The one who listens
The one who guides
Teaches
& protects.

The one who
Sacrifices
The one whose
Sure reward
Is love.

Dear Aneta,
The world
Of women
Would be
Hopeless
Without sisters
Like you.

We would go
Hungry
We would be
Empty
We would be
Cold
Shaky on our
Small, unsure legs
Without
Big sisters
Like you.

Your presence
In our
World
Is like
The sun
Warming us.

Like the
Blossoming trees
Feeding us
With the beauty
Of your willingness

To endure
To love us
Unconditionally
To give.

And so
On this day
That you
Reach the age
When mystics
& revolutionaries
Strike out
Into the
Wilderness
To begin
Their
Ministries
To a broken
World
& wise women
Quietly support
& champion
The beloved spirits
In their midsts
I salute
You
With love
& appreciation.

Thank you
For
Your patient
Loving

Heart
Your loyalty
& true
Devotion
To a little
Sister
Who needs
It
As she brings
Into being
Music
That honors
& uplifts
Life.

You are
The sister
Of all our dreams
Of sisterhood.

May all
Your years
Reflect
The loveliness
& magnitude
Of your
Great
Heart.

The Same as Gold

Now that I
Understand
That grief
Emotionally speaking
Is the same
As gold
I do not despair
That we are
All of us
Born to grieve.

There was a
Small dark
Girl
In my dream
The other night;
She had been
Left with me
By strange women
On their way
Somewhere
Else.

Taking her into
My arms
Into my house
Which had no roof

My tears
Covered us
Like rain.

My Friend Calls

My Friend Calls

My friend
Calls
From her front porch
That overlooks
The ocean.
She is sitting
In her sky
Chair
Her feet
Up
Watching
The world
Go by.

How I love
The joy
Ringing
In her voice
The satisfaction
I feel
In her smile.

She calls
Because
Gospel music
Is on the air
Where she

Lives
Angels
Are on her mind.

Coming Back from Seeing Your People

Coming back
From seeing your people
You were
So wonderfully
Full
Of yourself.

But now
You have supped
With vampires
They have fed
Feasted
On you.

They arise
Bright-eyed
Fit.

You alone have lost
Not only
Your sleep
But also
Your glow
The luster of
Affection
Heart welcome
Your people

Sent home
With you.

Beloved
You must learn
To walk alone
To hold
The precious
Silence
To bring home
And keep the precious
Little
That is left
Of yourself.

Someone I Barely Know

Someone I barely know
Except he used to
Make me smile
Slipped another woman
& her odd furniture
Into my house.

It was roomy enough
For two
& she was vaguely
Familiar.

Still, she was not a tenant
I chose myself
& her dining room
Table & chairs
Though a rich blue
I like
Had the look
Of gouged plastic &
Tarnished chrome.

The man I barely know
Who used to be so tickling
But now walks
Without the old spring in his
Step
Was looking for
Important papers.

Of course I did not know
Where they were.

While we searched
& I pretended to care
(Though distracted by the almost familiar
Woman & her misplaced chest of drawers)
He mentioned his old friend
Steve
Who had stopped laughing
Some time ago.

Steve was only five years
Younger than me
Had a heart attack
& died
He said
Scrutinizing moldy documents
With an anxious frown.

He is forty-five, this man,
& has lost
His virility
It is this old passport
That he
Is looking for.

Forget about the strange woman moving in with me,
I thought.
May we dwell in peace!

To be happy
I said
One must laugh
One must walk
& then, almost
As an afterthought
(& meaning sex)
One must make love.

But I did not seem
Too sure of this.

Anyway. No documents appeared.

To walk, to smile,
These can be done
From a very early age
I said into his stricken face
But perhaps
In childhood
&
Again in old age
It is not necessary
In order
To be happy
To fuck.

Despite the Hunger

Despite
the hunger
we cannot
possess
more
than
this:
Peace
in a garden
of
our own.

My African

Last night
Early in the morning
Just as it began
To rain
And I became weary
Longing
For sleep
I dreamed
Of you.

African man,
African chin
Nose, eyes, lips
& hair.

Blue is your color
& so it was
In this dream
The blue of the ocean
We can see from
Your green house.

We were in bed
Together
And I was content
Entwined
With you.

On the other side of me
In the blue bed
With the blue
Disappearing walls
There was a second
African man
Younger, not fearless like you.
Decidedly more in need
Of my care.

Just for a moment
I embraced him. Feeling wedded
To you & knowing you are too sure
Of my love
To be jealous.

We were in conversation
With two other
Dreamers, sitting attentive,
Beside our bed.

A younger woman
Seeking to learn
From me &
A man in his prime
Still thinking it possible
To nail everything down.

Apparently our conversation was about Literature.

It is not about
Writing
But about living

I said in the face
Of the hammer
He brought.

How Different You Are

How different
you are
from me.

A Portuguese
pirate
is hiding
in your curls.

Your skin
is bronzed
as ancient
gold.

You smell of mango
wild tobacco
coconut
milk
& sea.

All the things
I like.

New House Moves

New House Moves

I dreamed
Last night
That I had moved
Into a roomy new house.

How many new houses
Have I moved into?
And isn't there
Something always
Behind
These new house
Moves?

When I was a child
We moved each year
My parents
Working hard
Making nothing
For themselves
Except decency
That went
To the bone.

Now
In and out of dreams
I am always
Moving.

Finding shacks
& rundown
Houses
Fixing them up
& then moving
On.

In the dream
I said
To the silver-haired professor
Who introduced me
To the Communist Manifesto:
In this new house
I am going to paint
One of the rooms
Red!

It will probably be
A small room
He said
Laughing. In such a large
House.

How am I to live
In such prosperity?

Sharing everything
Still
My cup
Overflows
& I receive more
It appears to me
Than I ever give.

Poverty never prepared me
For this wealth.

Or to live
In the houses
My parents
Stubbornly
Dreamed.

Trapdoors to the Cellar
Spring-Grass Green

In this new house
Of many colors
Mauve and blue
Magenta and lilac
With trapdoors
To the cellar
Spring-grass green
I came upon
A room
Large, all white
With pleated doors
And a bed
Curving the length
Of the long wall.

My brother
Whom I had feared
Was moving in.

He stood there
Philosophical
Explaining the room
To me.

It had been
The room
Where all the junk
Was thrown

Especially those items
Tossed from
The renovation
Of many toilets
(Hence the row at one end of what used to be
toilet doors).

Now he said
He would claim
It as
His own.
In fact
He lived there
Already.

His only possession:
A quilt
That resembled
A map
Its destinations
Not easy
To read.

It is beautiful
I said.
And it was:

A fresh vision
Of a room. Spacious, light.
Nothing much in it
Every angle new.

At the end
Of the long room

That smelled of plaster
And newly opened paint
There hung a white
Antique
Cookstove
The most appealing
Art.

Why is it upside down
I asked
Though I admired it
As it was. And was thinking
Too
What a long time
It takes some of us
To cook.

Like some periods of Life
It works better
Upside down
He said.

And indeed
I realized
Enjoying
Him
At last
It had already
Worked
On me.

Whiter Than Bone

Last night
I dreamed
I was in
A fine
New house
Whiter than bone inside
With tall
Blue windows
Etched
In ancient
Art

I had forgotten
I was supposed
To be
Somewhere else
Speaking to a band
Of musicians
Whose name
I couldn't
Pronounce.

Lucky for me
A woman
Appeared
Who kept track
Of such things.

Off I went
To do my
Duty
Passing
Water spirits
Holding
Dog-face
Boys
On the way.

The woman
Who keeps track
Stopped to chat.
I noticed
The thick
Hair on
One little face
Was starting
To lift.

I saw that
I am passing
Out of a life
That kept me covered
& leaving it
With
The one who keeps track
To hold.

Even When I Walked Away

i

There were odd
New flowers
In a vase
Beside the door
The door
To my strange
New underground
There in the
Semi-dark
They sparkled
Like
Blue
Jewels.

Even when I
Walked away
Explored other
Rooms of
The new and spacious house
They beckoned me.

Come, they said
We are strange
We are new
We did not grow
Overnight
Although it is

Just now
That you see
Us
And we are yours.

Red Petals Sticking Out

ii

I could not accept
That such strange
Enchanting blossoms
Belonged to me.
Wearing my loosest coat
I snuck into my own
Dim foyer
And stole
A portion
Of the generous
Bouquet.
Sneaking it
Through the street
Concealed but poorly
Against my chest
Red petals
Sticking out
I came upon my other
Doors.

Inside My Rooms

iii

Inside my rooms
I began to mix them
With the flowers
I already had
The too familiar
Snapdragon
The overly sniffed
Daffodil
The hollyhock
Ho-hum.

A woman who
Did not love
Herself
Passed by
As I shaped
This new
Bouquet.
She said: I'm leaving.

I did not know
She was still
Inside my house.

Let Change Play God

Refrigerator Poems

While visiting a friend I wrote these poems using words I found on magnets scattered across the front of her refrigerator.

i

Let
Change
Play
God.

ii

Morning
Storm
Essential
Worship
Listen.

iii

Cloud
Said
To flower
Rain.

Just at Dusk

Just at dusk
I ventured out
Beyond my street
Two tawny cats
Waist high
Ran out to greet me
Or so I thought.

Sticking out
My hand
To pat
The larger one
I looked into its
Eyes and saw it intended
To eat me up.

Is this always
Where the lure
Of wildness
Leads?

Blood on the trail
The hand of the seeker vanished
Down some "tame"
Creature's throat?

The Moment I Saw Her

The moment
I saw her
Looked upon
Her
Without
Fear
& to admire
Her many
Legs
& her beauty
Only

In that
Moment
The
Entire
History
Of basket making
Was revealed
To me.

The old ones
Would have
Studied
Her.
They would have
Started with
Reeds

In a circle
Like
Her body
& kept them
Going
From leg
To
Leg
Weaving in
& out
Until
They were done.

I am connected
To all
Of this
By
My great
Grandmother's Native
Name
Tallulah, i.e.,
Basket maker,
Which
Turning fifty
I began claiming
As
My own
As I claim
My kinswoman
Spider &
The brilliant
Ancestral

Body
Of
Her art.

A Native Person
Looks up from the Plate

(Or, owning how we must look to a
person who has become our food)

They are eating
Us.
To step out of our doors
Is to feel
Their teeth
On our throats.

They are gobbling
Up our
Lands
Our waters
Our weavings
& our artifacts.

They are nibbling
At the noses
Of
Our canoes
& moccasins.

They drink our oil
Like cocktails
& lick down
Our jewelry
Like icicles.

They are siphoning
Our songs.

They are devouring
Us.
We brown, black,
Red, and yellow
Unruly
white
Morsels
Creating Life
Until we die:
Spread out in the chilling sun
That is
Their plate.

They are eating
Us raw
Without sauce.

Everywhere we
Have been
We are no more.
Everywhere we are
Going
They do not want.
They are eating
Us whole.
The glint of their
Teeth
The light

That beckons
Us to table
Where only they
Will dine.

They are devouring
Us.
Our histories.
Our heroes.
Our ancestors.
And all appetizing
Youngsters
To come.

Where they graze
Among the
People
Who create
Who labor
Who live
In beauty
And walk
So lightly
On the earth—
There is nothing
Left.

Not even our roots
Reminding us
To bloom.

Now they have wedged
The whole

Of the earth
Between their
Cheeks.

Their
Wide bellies
Crazily
Clad
In stolen
Goods
Are near
To bursting
With
The fine meal
Gone foul
That is us.

The Anonymous Caller

The anonymous caller
Begins
His diatribe
You shitty
Bitch
&
Ends it
With
A threat:
I Know
Where
You
    Live.

I can tell
By his
Voice
That he is
Young
&
Unaware
That
    As far
As Calamity
Is concerned
As far
As Death
Is concerned
All of us

Share
The same
Address;
All
Of us
Live
In the
Same
House.

I Was So Puzzled by the Attacks

I was so
Puzzled
By
The attacks.
It was as if
They believed
We were
In a race
To succeed
&
Someone
Other
Than
Death
Was at
The
Finish
Line.

At First, It Is True,
I Thought There Were Only Peaches &
Wild Grapes

To my delight
I have found myself
Born
Into a garden
Of many fruits.

At first, it is true,
I thought
There were only
Peaches & wild grapes.
That watermelon
Lush, refreshing
Completed my range.

But now, Child,
I can tell you
There is such
A creature
As the wavy green
Cherimoya
The black loudsmelling
& delicious
Durian
The fleshy orange mango
And the spiky, whitehearted
Soursop.

In my garden
Imagine!
At first I thought
I could live
On blue plums
That fresh yellow pears
Might become
My sole delight.

I was naïve, Child.

Infinite is
The garden
Of many fruits.
Tasting them
I myself
Spread out
To cover
The earth.

Savoring each &
Every
One—date, fig, persimmon, passion fruit—
I am everywhere
At home.

May 23, 1999

There is nothing
To say
I am content.
Zelie
On her blue bike
Has gone off
To feed
The dogs.

Reverend E. in Her Red Dress

Rev. E.
In her red dress
White hair
Shining
Black skin
Glowing
Standing at the door
Of our History
Standing at the gateway
To
Whatever lies
Ahead.

We see you
At last for who you truly are:
Daughter, Sister, Woman, Lover,
Mother, Friend
Your thoughts
Leaping
Silver
As fish
Brilliant as fire
Your laughter
Like your sorrow
A flashing
Stream
From which
We drink.

We see you
& know you reflect
The Divine Mother
She who gives birth
To all
And destroys all
At the end.

If we lived in
India
We would
Worship you
There, pilgrims
Stay gone
Wear rags
Eat handouts
Lock their hair
Pray beside
Rivers, holy stones
& shrines
Begging the Universe
For a single glimpse
Of you.

Divine Mother representing
The Life Force
The Earth
And all that She
Brings forth

Keep on praying
For us

Earth's children
That you
So clearly
Love

Help us to
Love one another
To shed our fears
Of unworthiness
Our habits
Of self-hatefulness
Our greed
To be accepted
As something
Other than
What we are.

Divine Mother
Keep on praying
For us
All Earthlings
All children
Of this awesome
Place
Not one of us
Knowing
Why we're here
Except to Be.

Keep on praying for us.

Your children
The children of Earth

Are starving
For the sight
Of something
Real
Dying for the sound
Of something
True.

Pray for us
To know
That nothing
Stops a lie
Like being
Yourself.

For Rev. Eloise Oliver, minister of the East Bay
Church of Religious Science, Oakland, California

All the People
Who Work for Me
& My Dog Too

All the People Who Work for Me
& My Dog Too

All the people who work for me
& my dog too
Think
I'm crazy
Rushing to
& fro
Doing this
& that
Never really
Still
Until
I absolutely
Sit.

They think
These people
Who work for me
& my dog
Too
That I have
Lost
My mind.

I'm always sending them
On errands
I could do
Myself.

My dog sometimes
Fetching a ball
Looks at me
With such pity
In her brown eyes.

My cat
Enduring the madness
No longer
Bailed out;
Went to live
With an aunt.

I feel myself
Slowly
Coming awake
In the rush.
Seeing the gingko tree
When it waves
Responding to seduction
By tomato
Noticing
José's mustache
& eyes
When I ask him
To fly
Down
The mountain
For an egg.

The Snail Is My Power Animal

While I was visiting the Amazon, a giant snail crawled uphill to lie in the doorway of my *tambo* (hut) every morning. According to shamanic wisdom, the animal who comes to you at least four times while you are on a medicine quest is your power animal.

That's the thing
About poems
You never know
When
They're going to crawl up
The hill
Stick out their wrinkled
Necks
& rest in your
Front door.

I was just here
Feeling
Overdressed
That I am
Too warm
Yet craving
Hot soup.

Between the
Boiling
Of the soup
& the tasting

Of it
I see my dog
Shift her body
Wondering why we're always
On the road
I see the house
I've made
Substantial
Solid
That I carry on my back
Like a shell.

In Everything I Do

In everything I do
There is an animal.
A cat, a dog
A snake
A bird
Or a chameleon.
An elephant
A turtle
A chicken or
A mouse.
The monkey
Is my special
Love
My totem
Ever since
I was born
& they commented
How much
I resembled
One.
Then I grew up
To learn
How very
Clever
Intelligent
Wise
Funny
& sweetly
Beautiful

The monkey
Is
& how
It is tortured.

The Writer's Life

During those times
I possess the imagination to ignore
The chaos

I live
The writer's life:
I lie in bed
Gazing out
The window.

To my right
I notice
My neighbor
Is always painting
And repainting
His house.
To my left
My other neighbor
Speaks of too much shade
Of tearing
Out
Our trees.

Sometimes
I paint
My house
Orange & apricot
Butterscotch & plum—
Sometimes

I speak up
To save
The trees.

The days
I like best
Have
Meditation
Lovemaking
Eating scones
With my lover
In them.
Walks on the beach
Picnics in the
Hammock
That overlooks
The sea.
Hiking in the hills
Leaning on
Our
Walking sticks.

Writers perfect
The art
Of doing nothing
So beautifully.

We know
If there is
A butterfly
Anywhere
For miles
Around

It will come
Hover
& maybe
Land
On our head.

If there is a bird
Even flying aimless
In the next
County
It will not only
Appear
Where we are
But sing.

If there is
A story
It will
Cough
In the middle
Of our
Lazy
Day
Only once
Maybe more
& announce
Itself.

Grace

Grace
Gives me a day
Too beautiful
I had thought
To stay indoors
& yet
Washing my dishes
Straightening
My shelves
Finally
Throwing out
The wilted
Onions
Shrunken garlic
Cloves
I discover
I am happy
To be inside
Looking out.
This, I think,
Is wealth.
Just this choosing
Of how
A beautiful day
Is spent.

Loss of Vitality

Loss of vitality
Is a sign
That
Things have gone
Wrong.

It is like
Sitting on
A sunny pier
Wondering whether
To swing
Your feet.

A time of dullness
Deadness
Sodden enthusiasm
When
This exists
At all.
Decay.

You wonder:
Was I ever "on"
Bright with life
My thoughts
Spinning out
Confident
As
Sunflowers?

Did I wiggle
My ears
& jiggle my toes
From sheer
Delight?

Is the girl
Grinning fiercely
In the old photo
Really me?

Loss of vitality
Signals emptiness
But let
Me tell you:
Depletion can be
Just the thing.

You are using
Have used
Up
The old life
The old way.

Now will rush in
The energetic,
The flexible,
The unmistakable
Knowing
That life *is* life
Not mood.

Until I Was Nearly Fifty

Until I was
Nearly fifty
I barely thought

Of age.

But now
As I approach
Becoming
An elder
I find I want
To give all
That I know
To youth.

Those who sit
Skeptical
With hooded
Eyes
Wondering
If there really
Is
A path ahead
& whether
There really
Are
Elders
Upon it.

Yes. We are there
Just ahead
Of you.

The path you are on
Is full of bends
Of crooks
Potholes
Distracting noises
& insults
Of all kinds.
The path one is on
Always is.

But there we are
Just out of view
Looking back
Concerned
For you.

I see my dearest
Friend
At fifty-one
Her hair
Now
An even
Steel.
She blushes much
& talks
Of passion.
It cannot be
For the bourgeois
Husband

I never
Liked.

I thought life
With him
Had killed
The wild-haired girl
I knew.

But no.
There she is.
There she goes.
Blushing.
Eldering.

I too talk
Stunned
Of love
Passion
Grace of mating
At last
With
My soul's
Valiant twin.

Oh youth!

I find
I do not
Have it in
My heart
To let
You stumble

On this curve
With fear.

Know this:

Surprise alone
Defines
This time
Of more than growth:
Of distillation
Ripeness
Enjoyment
Of being
On the vine.

Thanks for the Garlic

Thanks for the Garlic

For Susan

Thanks for the garlic,
I think I'm going
To plant
It now

Not wait
For spring.

The bulbs are
So fresh
And white
Their skins
So tight.

I love it
That you did
Not want to send
Them in anything
That would
Crush
Them. Though
Crushing
Is likely
Surely
To be
Their offspring's
Fate.

That you waited
To find
The perfect
Box.

Do you understand
How like you
This is?

There they sit
A smartly demure
Row
On the counter
Near the door
That leads
To the beginning
Of their future
Lives;
Fiery at heart,
You say.

Four hardy
Garlic
Souls
Unrepentant
Of their inner
Flame
Serenely
Awaiting
My gardener's
Pleasure
Of time
And place

Unabashed
By whatever's
To come

Cool

As nuns.

The New Man

You are the kind
Of man
Who makes
Me think
I want
A husband
Someone
To warm
My feet
At night
& who loves
To give me
Shoulder
Rubs
Someone
Who likes
To kiss
My fingers
And
My neck.

You do not
Say
Appalled:
What! You've made love
To other
Women?

You say
Instead:
All your life
You wanted
Your sisters
Your mother
& women everywhere
To be
Happy.

You do not say:
What is that
Weeping
Stranger
Doing
Sleeping
Late
At your house
Again?

You say:
Do you need
Help
With this one
Too?

Can I go for
Fresh water
How about
Food?

What Will Save Us

The restoration to the cow
Of her dignity.

The restoration to the pig
Of his intelligence.

The restoration to the child
Of her sacredness.

The restoration to the woman
Of her will.

The restoration to the man
Of his tenderness.

My Friend Arrived

For June

My friend arrived
Heartbroken
But wearing
Fresh
Smiles
As she unpacked
Bags
& furniture
Too
From the back
Of a white
Convertible.

Her presence
In our house
Although
On
So distant
A floor
You nor I
Ever
Ventured
Near it
Caused you
To feel
Our house
Was

No longer
Your home.

O husband mine
If you thought
I would forsake
Even one
Friend
For you
No matter
How crazy
You were
Mistaken.

The key to my heart
I give back
To you
The key
To
Your house.

Dead Men Love War

Dead Men Love War

Dead men
Love war
They sit
Astride
The icy bones
Of
Their
Slaughtered horses
Grinning.

They wind
Their
Pacemakers
Especially
Tight
&
Like Napoleon
Favor
Green velvet
Dressing
Gowns
On the
Battle
Field.

They sit
In board
Rooms
Dreaming of

A profit
That
Outlives
Death.

Dead men
Love war
They like to
Anticipate
Receptions
& balls
To which
They will bring
Their loathsome
Daughters
Desolation & decay
They like
To fantasize
About
The rare vintage
Of blood
To be
Served
&
How much company
They are going
To have.

Thousands of Feet Below You

Thousands of feet
Below you
There is a small
Boy
Running from
Your bombs.

If he were
To show up
At your mother's
House
On a green
Sea island
Off the coast
Of Georgia

He'd be invited in
For dinner.

Now, driven,
You have shattered
His bones.

He lies steaming
In the desert
In fifty or sixty
Or maybe one hundred
Oily, slimy
Bits.

If you survive
& return
To your island
Home
& your mother's
Gracious
Table
Where the cup
Of lovingkindness
Overflows
The brim
(&
From which
No one
In memory
Was ever
Turned)

Gather yourself.

Set a place
For him.

Living off of Isolated Women

Living off of isolated
Women
Is the easiest
Work
In the world.

Tell them
You climbed
The mountain
Just to see them.
Tell them their wisdom
Means the moon
& the stars
To you.

Tell them
Their money
Buys
Them more
Of this.

They Made Love

They made love
On the altar
Of the church
In which
She received
First Communion.

It was the middle
Of the night
An old
Almost blind
Aunt
Best friend of
Her ancient
Grandmother
Happened
To drive
Past.

The bride in
Process
Her long gown
Crushed into the
Flowers
On which she lay
Rose
To go out
& talk
To her.

While the groom
In regal tux
Washed her hands
In the holy water
Laced with
Champagne.

It is a ceremony, she explained
To the old woman
Who seemed
Relieved
To believe her.

It is
A wedding.

It is an honest
Way
To become
Married
To
The church.

To Be a Woman

To Be a Woman

To be a woman
Does not mean
To wear
A shroud;

The Feminine
Is not
Dead
Nor is she
Sleeping

Angry, yes,
Seething, yes.

Biding her time;

Yes.
Yes.

Thanksgiving

Everything that
Has welcomed
You
Has paid
A price.

You want now
To play
With dolphins.

Your excuse:

They think
They want
To play
With
You.

The Last Time I Left
Our House

The last time I left
Our house
You were sitting
On the stoop
Smiling.

Your new girlfriend
Had decked
You out
In brand-new
Khaki shorts
A rosy

Peachy
Shirt
& stout
Intrepid
Sandals.

Your wavy
Hair and
Wavering eyes
Bespoke
A forlorn
Anticipation.

Not for me
For us

Would
You have
Dressed
This way
Or taken
A precious weekend
Off
From work.

I am on my way
Somewhere too
My companion
No lover
An enormous
Milkmaid
Who has promised
To drag
Me
Bleeding
Through the armpits
& groin
Of lower
Europe:
Yugoslavia,
Turkey,
Crete.

The house that
We have
Made
For us
Is perfect.

I turn,
Passing your
Blindly
Smiling
Face
& see its
Grandeur
How it rises
Behind us
Serene &
Granite
Like
A cliff.

In a flash
I see how you
Could duck
The sharklike woman
Zooming
Even now
Toward the entrance
Of
Our street.

How I could
Tell the huge
Milkmaid
I do not care
To see
The sights
That she discerns

My bloody
Internal
Landscape

Is enough.

I picture us
Suddenly
Remembering
Our life
& who indeed
We still are
Waking from
This awful trance
In time
To stop
The inexorable
Flow
Time turned
Suddenly liquid
Though glacial
Slow.

I see you rise
&
I
Smiling myself
Now
Take your
Hand
As we go
Backward
Through

Those ornate
Massive
Doors
That
Reminded us
Of eternity
And cost
Us so much
To refurbish
To repair.

We back in.

Toward bedroom
Or kitchen

Parlor floor
Or den

Or toward
Those prismed
Bay
Windows
We loved
That almost
Faced
The bay.

Backing in.

With nothing
To say.

I Loved You So Much

I loved you
So much
That when
You left
It took
A lot
To keep me
Alive.

Prayer helped. And giving
Myself over
To emptiness.

Years later
I sit
On this
Beach
Not far
From an old
Hawaiian
Kahuna
Who teaches
All and sundry
How to clean
Their bowels.

Don't
Hold on
To the Old

Stuff, flush it out
She says
Leis to her
Ears
Perched
Like a diva
On her bright yellow
Porch.

I gaze
Thankfully at the sea
Time's most faithful
Clock
Amazed
That every trace
Of that
Old pain
Your leaving
Stuffed me
With
Is washed
Clean.

Winning

The smallest child
Understands:

Anyone who terrorizes us
Is a terrorist;

Anyone who steals from us
Is a thief;

Any one who loves
Has won.

Falling Bodies

On September 11, 2001, several domestic planes were hijacked; the planes were then used as bombs—flown into the World Trade Center in New York City and into the Pentagon, in an attempt to destroy them. The attack on the World Trade Center destroyed the World Trade Towers, two of the tallest buildings in the world. As the towers burned, people were seen leaping from their windows.

Falling Bodies

He told me
Some of them were holding hands
Leaping from
The flaming
Windows.

To these ones
Leaping, holding hands
Holding
Their own
I open
My arms.

Everything
It is
Necessary
To understand
They mastered
In the last
Rich
Moments

That
They owned.

There is no more
To learn
In life
Than this:
How to
Love and
How not to miss
To waste
The moment
Our understanding
Of this
Is clear.

We are
Each other's
Own
Near and far
Far and wide
(Even if we leap
Into loving
In such haste
It is certain
There will remain
Nothing of us
Left.)

Consider: The pilot
& the
Hijacker

Might
Have been
Holding
Hands.

Those who wish
To make
A war
Of this
Will never believe
It possible.

But how enlightenment
Comes
To others
We may never
Know
Or even
How
Someday
It may come
To us.

*And
If it does not come
In this lifetime
We may be hopeful
For the next.*

When he tells me
This story
I look

Deep
Into my beloved's
Ear.

It is a finely
Curved
Surprisingly
Small
Fleshy-on-the-
Lower-outside
Miracle.

On the inside
Hairy, growing its own
Wax
It can hear!

A love of bodies
Sweeps
Over me.

And of
Soul.

Why the War You Have in Mind
(Yours and Mine) Is Obsolete

The brain
Though encased
In separate
Heads
Is
One brain.

Dropping a bomb
On
One head
Or one million
Is perceived
By all the rest
(Of brain, if not of heads)
To be a
Threat
Not
Definitely not
So smart
It is
An end.

Projection

To start
You must divulge
Not a secret
But a thing
Not commonly
Known:

That at the back
Of each human's eyeballs
Resides the image
Of a little child.

It is the world
Child
& it sits
There
Gravely, looking
Out
Of
Our
Eyes
Waiting
For us
To
Understand.

So tell him this
First of all.

Then
When he says
Those Indians
Are remote
Savages, who do not deserve
Their own forest
Tell him: All the children of the Earth
Are perfect.

When he says: Those Germans
& their ovens
Tell him: Like clouds, or grains of sand, all the children of
the Earth
Are perfect.

When he says
Those rotten Arabs
& their
Women in
Bedsheets
You tell him: All the children of the Earth
Are perfect.

When he says
Those Chinese
& their
Femicide
You say: Like the feet of Jesus, the eyelashes of
the Buddha, all the children of the Earth
Are perfect.

It is our Life Work
To liberate across the planet

The world child
Who always
Lives
Behind
Our eyeballs
Imprisoned
In the only
Image (our own)
We can
(Sometimes)
See.

This poem expands to hold almost all countries and
nationalities: When he says
Those Israelis & their
Concentration Camps
Those Americans &
Their Genocide
Those Africans &
Their holocausts
You still say: All the children
Of the Earth
Are
Perfect.

When You Look

You do not want
To believe
Someone
Who tells
You
When you look
At the sky
That you see
A place
With couches
For the weary
& thronelike
Chairs of rest.

Someone, serene, saved
Playing listless harp.

Many of the formerly
Fallen
Well fed
Jolly at last
Driving
White
Cadillacs.

You do not need
To believe
Someone who does not
Want it known

That heaven
Is a matter
Not of inventing
Glory
But of recognizing
It.
That the blue sky with its
Sunsets &
Clouds
Is simply
Beautiful. And that is enough.

You do not need to follow
Someone who
Does not want it known
That we are all
Equal to God
If we keep
Our eyes
(And our hearts)
Open.

The Tree

The Tree

The tree
Was so large
I could not see
The top of it
So wide I could not see
The ends
Of it.
It was the world
Tree
& it had
Presented itself
To me.

José the shaman
Said:

My people used
To dream
A tree
All of us
Together. We
Dreamed
The same
Tree.
It reached from
Heaven to earth
Earth to heaven
And it sang.

But now
He said
Our people are
Dying
Many are sick
Many are scattered
The rainforest
Is being
Cut down.

The tree does
Not come
To us
It does not
Sing
To us
Anymore.

But it has
Come
Perhaps
To me
I said
& told him
About the tree.

It was so large
I do not know
How
It managed
To get
Inside my dream.
Though it did not

Sing
Except
In
Awesomeness.

Now I understand
& said this
To
José: Though it is the world tree
& larger than the world
It was afraid to sing aloud.
It was looking
For shelter
Even in
My
Small space.

The Climate of the Southern Hemisphere

The climate
My body
Appreciates
Has
Moisture
& has
Sun
My hair
In this climate
Bushes out
My nails
Turn sleek
& smooth
My lips
Never crack
My bones
Never ache.

We are made
For each other
The Southern
Hemisphere's climate
& me.

The joy of sweating
Of eating fruit
Handpicked
From cool &

Patient
Trees
The warmth
Of the earth
—& I know
I do not want
A casket—
That promises
To melt
All of me
Someday
Into
Its verdant
Self.

In this climate
The smell
Of ants
Is the scent
Of rain.

Just so
(Only here)
Are important messages
Delivered.

Where Is That Nail File?
Where Are My Glasses?
Have You Seen My Car Keys?

Nothing is ever lost
It is only
Misplaced
If we look
We can find
It
Again
Human
Kindness.

My Ancestors' Earnings

My Ancestors' Earnings

For over a decade
My ancestors
Earned for me
Over a
Million dollars
A year.

With our righteous loot
We bought
For me
Every house
We truly
Loved
Every car
& work
Of art in earlier times
(Laboring, laboring
Over uncleared fields
& kitchen floors
That had no end)
Drenched in
Sweat
We were
Denied.

Now, sated
We rest.

Looking about us
We see
We have been feeding
The little ·
Child
Who wanted Things
For several
Centuries
& did not
Have them.

Wanted a mother
Separate
From her enslavement
Whether by field
Domestic service
Or her own art

Wanted a world
Cut off
From
Its
Woes

Wanted
In two words
Pleasure
&
Security.

But now begins
The downward
Slide.

It will all
Be over
Soon
All the wanting
Of this thing
& that
That drives
This plane.

I can let go.

Of houses
& of cars
Of art
& of
Artifacts. No material
Object
Will seem
Of relevance
Anymore.

I can let go!

Free-falling into
The very
Arms
That held me as
I shopped, the very arms
That worked
The broom
The machete
& the hoe.

My Friend Yeshi

My friend Yeshi
One of the finest
Midwives
Anywhere
Spent a whole
Season
Toward
The middle
Of her life
Wondering
What to do
With herself.

I could not
Understand
Or even
Believe
Her quandary.

Now
Thank goodness
She is over it.
Women come to her
Full
Babies drop
To her
Hand.

It is all
Just the way
It is.

Sometimes
Life seizes
Up
Nothing stirs
Nothing flows
We think:
Climbing
This rough
Tree
&
All the time
The rope looped
Over
A rotten
Branch!

We think:
Why did I choose
This path
Anyway?
Nothing at
The end
But sheer cliff
& rock-filled
Sea.

We do not know
Have no clue

What more
Might come.

It is the same
Though
With Earth:
Every day
She makes
All she can
It is all
She knows it is all
She can possibly
Do.

And then, empty, the only
Time She is flat, She thinks: I am
Used up. It is winter all the time
Now. Nothing much to do
But self-destruct.

But then,
In the night, in
The darkness
We love so much
She lies down
Like the rest of us
To sleep
& angels come
As they do
To us
& give her
Fresh dreams.
(They are really always the old ones, blooming further.)

She rises, rolls over, gives herself a couple of new kinds of
grain, a few dozen unusual flowers, a playful spin on the
spider's web called the internet.

Who knows
Where the newness to old life
Comes from?
Suddenly
It appears.
Babies are caught by hands they assumed were always
waiting.
Ink streaks
From the
Pen
Left dusty
On
The shelf.

This is the true wine of astonishment:

We are not
Over
When we think
We are.

Ancestors to Alice

Forget about trying
To keep all
The pretty houses
Going;

These are only
The toys
We gave you
Because
In you
We felt
We deserved
To play.

Enough. We
Have grown up
Living on
Here
In the so-called
Afterlife.

Your true work
Is to
Remember us
To sing our names
Recount
Or even record
Our deeds

Laugh at
Our jokes.

Your true work
Is to notice
The big feet
Of the
95-year-old
Midwife
From Alabama
To feel
In your body
How long
She has
Stood
On them.
To hold them
In your hands
Stroking &
Soothing
Until
You
Can rest.

One of the Traps

One of the worst traps
Is finding yourself
Despising someone
Really good.

There they are
Wearing a miniskirt
Talking dirty
But washing
The filthy
Feeding the hungry
Defending
The poor
Befriending the dead

& all you can
Say in your
Defense

Is
Their bleached hair
& studded
Nostril
Hardly goes
With so much
Leg.

Not Children

Not Children

War is no
Creative response
No matter
The ignorant
Provocation
No more
Than taking
A hatchet
To your
Stepfather's
Head
Is
Not to mention
Your husband's.

It is something
Pathetic
A cowardly
Servant
To base
Emotions
Too embarrassing
To be spread out
Across the
Destitute
Globe.

The only thing
We need

Absolutely
To leave
Behind
Crying
Lonely
In
The dust.

You Can Talk

You can talk about
The balm in Gilead
But what about
The balm
Right
Here

What about
The healing of
The wounded heart
When someone
You have harmed
Gleefully
Embraces you?

Goddess

I am so glad
I can recognize
A goddess
When I see one.

There is Yeshi's
Trustworthiness
Glenna's
Patience
Sue's willing helpfulness (& genius)
Zelie's
Wild
Laughter
& song
Evelyn's
Loyalty

Diana's equanimity

Ruth's incredible
Storytelling
& inexplicable

Suffering.

The scent of
My mother's
Roses.

What is needed

Is heart
Wisdom alone
To see this
Not—the added blessing—
Eyes.

Why War Is Never a Good Idea

(A Picture Poem for Children
Blinded in War)

Though War speaks
Every language
It never knows
What to say
To frogs.

Picture frogs
Beside a pond
Holding their annual
Pre–rainy season
Convention.

They do not see WAR
Huge tires
Of a
Camouflaged
Vehicle
About to
Squash
Them flat.

Though War has a mind of its own
War never knows
Who
It is going
To hit.

Picture a donkey
Peacefully
Sniffing a pile
Of straw.
A small boy
Holds
The end
Of its
Frayed
Rope
Bridle.

They do not see it
They are both thinking
Of dinner.
The boy
Is hoping for
Polenta & eggs
Maybe a carrot
Or apple
For
Dessert.

Just above
Them
Something dark
Big as
A car
Is
Dropping.

Though War has eyes
Of its own

& can see oil
&
Gas
& mahogany trees
& every shining thing
Under
The earth

When it comes
To nursing
Mothers
It is blind;
Milk, especially
Human,
It cannot
See.

Picture a woman
Beside a window.
She is blissful
Singing
A lullaby.
A baby twirls
A lock of her
Dark hair
Suckles
For all
It is
Worth.

They do not smell War
Dressed in
Green & brown

Imitating
Their fields
Marching slowly
Toward them
Up
The steep
Hill.

Though War is Old
It has not
Become wise.
It will not hesitate
To destroy
Things that
Do not
Belong to it
Things very
Much older
Than itself.

Picture the forest
With its
Rivers
& rocks
Its pumas
&
Its
Parakeets
Its turtles
Leopards
&
Snakes.

High above them War
Has turned itself
Into a white cloud
Trailing
An
Airplane
That
Dusts
Everything
Below
With
A powder
That
Kills.

War has bad manners.
War eats everything
In its path
& what
It doesn't
Eat
It
Dribbles
On:

Here
War is
Munching on
A village
Its missiles
Taking chunks

Big bites out
Of it.
War's
Leftover
Gunk
Seeps
Like
Saliva
Into
The
Ground.
It
Is finding
Its
Way
Into the
Village
Well.

War tastes terrible
& smells
Bad. It never
Considers
Body
Odor
Or
Weird
Side
Effects.
When added
To water

It makes
You sick
Sip by sip.

You could die
While
Choking
&
Holding
Your
Nose.

Now, suppose You
Become War.
It happens
To some of
The nicest
People
On earth:
& one day
You have
To drink
The
Water
In this place.

The Award

The Award

Though not
A contest
Life
Is
The award
& we
Have
Won.

Though We May Feel Alone

Though we may feel
Alone
We never
Really are.
The ancestors
The one called
God
&
The one called
Death
Prominent
Among them
Rest on our
Shoulders
Always.

It is as if
We carried two
Birds' nests
Just below
Our ears;
In these
Like so many eggs
The ancestors
Sit.

They ride along
Overhearing

Every conversation
Every
Thought
Watching everything
We do.

Fragile as eggs
But tough
Cookies
Too
It does not matter
To them
If we lose our
Way
On occasion
That we become
Lost
Or fall down.

Missteps are
Common
On every path
They've seen
(& they've seen lots!).

What matters to them
Is that
We right ourselves
Keep a better watch
Over where we're going
That they retain
The high view

They like
& what is most
Crucial
For helping us:
Balance.

When We Let Spirit Lead Us

When we let Spirit
Lead us
It is impossible
To know
Where
We are being led.
All we know
All we can believe
All we can hope
Is that
We are going
Home
That wherever
Spirit
Takes us
Is where
We
Live.

Dream

Sometimes
When I dream
About
My mother
She is in
One of the
Shacks
Her art
Made
Radiant.

She might
Be lying
All in pink
Just
In
The doorway
Sunlight
Warm
Upon her
Singing.

In Life,
A Methodist
Then an
Atonal
Jehovah's
Witness

My mother
Did not
Sing.

At least
Not the
Subversive
Jazzy
Melodies
She favors
In
My
Dream.

On my altar
For years
Two women's
Framed
Faces
Have inspired
Challenged
Nourished me
In every way:

(Although I had not noticed, before my dream, their
resemblance, as close as twins.)

One contained
Righteous
In her garden
My mother;
The other an Outlaw

In a smoky
Nightclub
Lady Day.

We Are All So Busy

We are all so busy.

We say: I am on fire
To see you
But next week
I'll be away
In Boston
& the
Week after that
I have
An important
Meeting
In Kalamazoo.

Ah, Kalamazoo.

A place
I spend
Far
Too much
Time in
Myself.

The Backyard, Careyes

The Backyard, Careyes

Lying grateful

Under a tree
Wind blows.

Yellow leaves
Cover me.

Gold

Leaf shower.

Practice

Though
Like you
I am awake
At least
Some
Of the
Time

Deep
Slumber is far
From
Unknown

I am
A
Practicing
Alice.

Dreaming the New World in Careyes

Every night
While
I dream
The New World
Right next door
All night long
A raucous
Gathering
Of idle
White
Men
Is intensely
Partying.

Their music
So loud
It more than
Hurts
My ears
It wounds
My heart.
Their cries of pleasure
So disdainful
Of my
Comfort
I pull the covers
Over my
Head.

They do not listen
When I advise
Stopping. They do not want
To acknowledge
I am
The shadow
That has always
Lived
Next door.

The changes in
The world
They sense
Rather
Than know. Yet they
& we
The dreamers
Are real.

Much of earth
Is enduring
This sleepless
Night.

The night
Of our
Transition.

Of bitter
Revelers, even their play
Turned to war—if only against
Their scribbling, sleepless
Neighbor—

Unhappy
But
Determined
To disrupt
The dream
Of peace.

Patriot

If you
Want to show
Your love
For America
Love
Americans
Smile
When you see
One
Flowerlike
His
Turban
Rosepink.

Rejoice
At the
Eagle feather
In a grandfather's
Braid.

If a sister
Bus rider's hair
Is
Especially
Nappy
A miracle
In itself
Praise it.

How can there be
Homeless
In a land
So crammed
With houses

&
Young children
Sold
As sex snacks
Causing our thoughts
To flinch &
Snag?

Love your country
By loving
Americans.

Love Americans.

Salute the soul
& the body
Of who we
Spectacularly &
Sometimes
Pitifully are.
Love *us*. We are
The flag.

Because Light Is Attracted to Dark

Because light is attracted
To dark
As dark is
To light
Let's face
It
You're
Fucked.

What can I tell
You
Lie back
&
Enjoy it.

You're about
To lose
That lockpicker
Nose
You
Always
Hated
The predator
Eyes
&
The
Stringy
Hair
You're always

Shaking out
In mixed
Company
To reassure
Yourself.

About
To lose
The
Unbecoming
Tendency
To strut into
Other peoples'
Lands
&
Claim
Everything
As your
Own
Except
The sweetness
Of dark
Angels
Welcoming
You
Home.

When Fidel
Comes to Visit Me

When Fidel Comes to Visit Me

Usually
When Fidel comes
To visit me
He helps with all the household
Chores. I am surprised and not surprised
To see him so at home
In my kitchen
Sweeping or mopping
The floor
Doing laundry and worrying
Out offensive smells
Lurking
In my *refrigerador*.

Sometimes he looks more like Ortega
Than like himself:
How do you make yourself
So short I ask
And brown
As well?

He shrugs. So tall responding
To this question
The tops of his shoulders
Are out of sight.

In my dreams I am an average size
And so I was last night.
Once again Fidel appeared

This time gray & much
Fatigued.
I put him and his aide
Who looked as tired as he
To bed at once. And I began
To sweep my house, mop my kitchen
Floor, clear my refrigerator
And pantry too
Of all unpleasantness.
While I was doing this
They slept.

And then
Just as I stood aside
Admiring my handiwork
(I had waxed and polished all the
Furniture & cooked paella as well!)
The two of them appeared:
The aide relaxed, and seeming
Somewhat
Fatter.
Fidel refreshed, looking about
For the gifts he'd
Brought as he'd staggered
Upon my porch
A night and a day
Ago;
Grinning
Showing all his teeth
Which seemed to be

All there
& wanting to dance.

In dreams it is said missing teeth signify loss of dignity
or "face." It is said Fidel cannot dance.

No Better Life

There is no better life
Than this
To let the good-looking
Gardener
Go home
Early
To his wife
& New baby.
To lie
On the blue couch
Recuperating
From a
Just
Battle.
To be full
Of soup
Cooked
By a friend.

Someone Should Have Taught You This

(Tenacatita Beach, Mexico)

When the vendor
Looks
Exhausted
& her skin
Is bad
When her body staggers
Stunted
By years of
Dragging
Somebody else's
Tawdry wares
Across
The sand

When her children
& she herself
Appear more
Shrunken
Each time
You see
Them
And the conquistador's
Mother Hubbard
Sets her apart
From all
Educational
Medical

Or
Even
Nutritional
Pursuits

When her very
Eyeballs
Shriek
Of injustice
& their
Whites
Are flushed
With blood

When you know
She has
Been on
Her feet
500 years

You should also know
Though greedy
To buy worthless
Trinkets
At half price
That
Today is
No time
To bargain.

Dream of Frida Kahlo

It was big.
It was a sea
Of shit.

Neither she
Nor I
Had any notion
What to do
With
It.

Our mothers came.

One resourceful
The other
Stout
& using
Just
Their thoughts
Soon they
Had contained
The odious
Ocean
In a pot
That
Was not only
Clean
But shining!

Standing over it
Slapping palms
They smiled
At us
Beloved daughters
Left
Suddenly
With much less
Work
To do.

Then
Like Cheshire
Cats
They disappeared
Their smiles
Like light
The crescent moon
Upon
Our foreheads.

Frida died
That night.
We laid her out
Well dressed
Of course
Beneath the star-
Bespeckled
Sky.

There was a cloud
For beauty
But even so

She was not under
It.

At dawn
All the roosters
In the world
Began to crow
& I
My arms widestretched
Raised
Her long dark
Braid
To greet
The sun.

To her funeral
Not only traveled
Diego
& many
Masters who
Had lived
Before
But also:
A long line
Of stately
Swaying
Elephants
Their images
Left behind
Them
Engraved in stone
Came slowly
Down

Gravely
Down
Emphatically
Down
To pay their respects
From the hills.

My Mother Was So Wonderful

My mother
Was so wonderful
I wanted
To marry
Her.

My father
Hapless
Never
Seemed
To notice
Her unmistakable
Glory
& let thirty
Years
Go by
Without
Be-ringing her.

How could
Such a fox
As she
Have fallen
In
With
Such
A
Clown?

Cheerfully
She wore
My ring
Though it turned green
Upon
Her finger.

I admired it
Often. The weak light
Of rhinestone
The cheap
Gleam
Of almost
Gold.

Proud
That
Such a Being
Magnificent
Beyond
My boldest
Imaginings
Consented
With a smile
To
Belong
To
Me.

Aging

Aging

Your job:

Every morning
To look
Into
The mirror

To note
In spite

Of everything

Life is humming
Along.

To say
In wonder
&
Fit
Anticipation:

There *it* is!

Aging. *Life.*

What has it done?
What's it doing now?
What is it going
To do?

Some Things to Enjoy
About Aging

The dignity
of
Silver:
New light
Around my
Head.

Forgetfulness:
So much less
To recall!

Talking to myself:
Amusing company
For me &
My dog.

Lying Quietly

Lying quietly
bones aching
I feel
I must
be
falling
through
them.
That standing
upright
was
an idea
an interlude
an illusion:
that we are
as always
on our way
to dust.

Wrinkles

Wrinkles
Invited by Life
Have
Entered
This house.

Someone
New
Is living
In my
Face.

Life Is Never Over

Life is never
Over
After this one
Begins
The journey
Of
Vegetation
Of being roses
Of being trees.
Only after much
Unhappiness
& many bad decisions
(So long a time
We need
Hardly
Even think
Of it)
Begins
The life
Of dumb metal:
Of being
Glancing
Axes
Whining saws
Rust-weary
Shears.

Bring Me the Heart
of María Sabina

If They Come to Shoot You

If they come to shoot you
and because you lived in
Mississippi
where so many
died
you know
they might:
Ask them first
to let you find
your hidden
picture
of
Che Guevara.

Place it just
at eye level
& if you cannot
find it
even after
they've
ransacked
your house
imagine
those eyes
bright &
steady
the calm of them
on that
last morning

in a poor
chilly
village
in Bolivia

His death offered
as a birthday
present
to a young man
so young & ignorant
that he took careful, prideful aim.

Meanwhile, El Che,
the schoolteacher
who gave him
his last supper
reports,
stood at ease
on his wounded leg
though he
had bled
steadily
through the long night.

His imperturbable idea
was to come back
after his escape
& build her
a proper school. (Perhaps it was this audacity
that caused them, later, to cut off his hands.)

With what compassion
he must
have gazed
at his young
murderer.

An assassin
kept
brutish &
illiterate
for just such
a purpose
as this.

Someone so
mulelike
we can almost hear
the whining
of incomprehension
thirty years
after
that fateful morning
as all
the *campesinos*
in his neighborhood
don't even
jeer at him
anymore
but simply
turn

their sun-withered
cheeks
away.

I too

pray for you
young, poor, ignorant
pathetic
assassin.

You have been sent by someone
who also
does not
understand.

& that is what
we can
remember
to do
pray
for them
when they come
for us.

You Too Can Look,
Smell, Dress, Act
This Way

Whenever I notice
advertising
How they can
tuck away your
nipples
&
suck off
your hips
& make you
smell
like nobody
who's ever
lived
I like to think
of Jane Goodall.

Plain Jane
Goodall.

I like
to imagine her
hunkered down
motionless
quiet
observant
of wild chimpanzees

in
the bush.

Her gray hair
tugged
off
her honest
face
—with a rubber
band
I'd bet—

While she studies
the body proud
cousins
looking for clues
about why
we're so
dissatisfied.

Sometimes
a person's name
just
suits
them.

Jane. Nothing
you can do
with Jane
except say it.
Goodall.

Advertising never
seems to reach
Jane. Her hips always appear
to be just
where they always
were. Her breasts
never
strain to declare
themselves.

Each time
she emerges blinking
out of
the mists
she's wearing
the exact
same
white blouse & indifferent
blue skirt.

She never seems
to have heard
of a makeup
that wasn't
character.

If I could
sniff
Jane Goodall
as her friends

the chimpanzees
do
I know
she would smell
just like
her name.

Like no advertiser's
perfume
ever touched
her
No surgeon's
shears
ever trimmed
such ample
integrity.

She would smell
like earth
air, water
ancient forest
&
like no man
was ever
there.

The Breath of the Feminine

Smoking
In boardrooms
Eating
Carrion
At thirty thousand
Feet

Still
Remember
Before foulness
Becomes
Inseparable
From air:

The breath
Of the Feminine
Is sweet.

Relying on neither man nor religion, accepting neither chador nor burka nor any form of premature shroud, whether physical or spiritual, and completely open to her own intense intimacy with the divine, María Sabina speaks to all people, all seekers, all healers, all lovers of earth, of this time.

Bring Me the Heart
of María Sabina

Life
You who have brought
Me
So many deep rivers
To cross
And as many sturdy
Boats
You who now bring me
To the curve
In the long road
That permits a view
Of the white roses
That bloom
Profusely
Beside
Death's door

Bring me the power
Of the Virgen de Guadalupe
The fearlessness
Of Martin
The resignation
Of Jesus
The wisdom of
Sofia
The equanimity of
Gandhi
The vastness

Of Yemaya
The insouciance
Of Kwan Yin
The joie de vivre
Of Buddha
The devotion &
In the end
Serenity
Of Che
Bring me the heart
Of María Sabina.

Bring me the heart
Of María Sabina
Matron saint
Of Mexico
Defender of tobacco
&
Of herb
Priestess of mushrooms.

It was a heart
Of humbleness
A heart of belief
A heart that rejoiced
In the recovered
Health
& happiness
Of
Every sufferer.

A heart that looked
To the earth

For help
In
Healing us
&
Found it.

Bring me the heart
Of María Sabina.

The first time
She ate
"The children"
As she called
The mushrooms
That would
Later heal
The multitudes
She was a child
Herself
& starving. They glowed white
In the grass
Like pieces
Of bread.
In the vision
She was given
She saw her dead
Father & what is more
Felt his protection
& his love.
A poor Indian
As she
His daughter
Was

The misery of life
Under conquest
Dispossession
Poverty
Humiliation
Had taken
His breath away.
Seeing him
Whole
Vibrant
Alive
In her vision
Hearing him
Speak
To her
María Sabina
Was healed of the misery
Of grieving his death
Of missing him. Her hunger
Likewise
Disappeared.

From that
Time on
She accepted
Earth's
Offering of
All healing
"Children," whether mushroom
Tobacco, or herb
As medicine

& with them
Treated
Healed
Cured
All who
Came
To her.
Accepting
That she could not
Bear to
Become rich
On what Earth
Gave for free
No one
Suffering
Was ever
Turned away.

Life paid her with more life.

O Life
Bring us the heart
Of María Sabina
Help us to trust
In you
Help us to
Honor
& enjoy
Your surprises
&
Use them

To help ourselves
& others
As she did.

To her small house
In the misty mountains
Of Mexico
Came
The high
& the low
Though none
Were high
Or low
To her
& she helped
Them all.

Bring me the heart
Of María Sabina.

An old woman
Still scrawny from
Her hungry youth
Her hair gray
Her eyes soft
Still on the path
Of healing
& Unconditional
Love
Until
She died.

And when she did
Leave them,

After cherishing
Them
Beyond their
Understanding
& having survived
All attacks
On her
Morals
&
Her state of
Mind
Her patience
And willingness to
Sit with their
Sickness
Never flagging
Mexicans everywhere
Lit their candles
& wept.

This is the heart
That belongs
In us
We
Also
"The children"
Indigenous
Like
The mushroom
The tobacco &
The herb
Indigenous
To this

Continent
This hemisphere
We wish to take
Only
What the earth
Offers
& wants
Freely
To give.
As it delights
Through every
Magic "child"
In reconnecting
Us to Itself.

Bring me the heart
Of María Sabina.

A heart inexplicable
In its generosity
Its lovingkindness
& its grace.

It is the heart
That is ours if we
Dare to claim it.

Americans of all
The Americas

Both Mother
& Father

Grandmother
& Grandfather
Guiding Spirit
Of this
Place.

About the Type

Minion is a 1990 Adobe Originals typeface by Robert Slimbach. Minion is inspired by classical, old-style typefaces of the late Renaissance, a period of elegant, beautiful, and highly readable type designs. Created primarily for text setting, Minion combines the aesthetic and functional qualities that make text type highly readable with the versatility of digital technology.